VIRTUE STORIES

Help is on the Way

Lalita Iyer

Om KIDZ
An imprint of Om Books International

Andre's mouth watered at the juicy mangoes hanging from the tree. It would be a matter of minutes to climb up, pluck a few of the choicest ones and then scamper down again.

He'd sprained his ankle playing football last week and the doctor had told him that he was not to play football for two weeks. But he hadn't said anything about climbing trees, Andre thought to himself.

The mango tree was his big secret.

It stood right at the end of a path with a dead end which no one frequented. The mystery lane was lined on both sides with the back walls of huge apartment complexes in which his friends lived.

He planned the route carefully - he'd need to climb just three of the branches to get to the mango that he had his eye on - a large, shiny, glossy orange-yellow one that hung so close, yet so far!

He swung himself higher and higher; and before he knew it, he had plucked his prize off its stem and sunk his teeth into it. Ah! The sweetness and juiciness of a mango fresh off the tree filled his mouth. He propped himself up against the slim bark and took his time enjoying it.

Andre was about to swing back down when he spotted an even larger, bigger prize a few branches up. His ankle had begun to feel a little sore and he knew it was best that he headed back home; but the sweetness of the mango filled his mouth and he swung himself up, up and away!

He was rewarded with not one but three gifts of goodness and at last, his tummy filled with the bliss of mangoes, he decided to descend. But a cool, strong breeze had begun to blow and every time he tried to find a footing on the thin branches below him, the branch swung away and his ankle began to pain a little bit more.

He tried again and again. But it was no good and his ankle now throbbed with a fierce pain.

The ground also seemed a long-long way away. Should he jump? But his ankle?

Should he stay put? And if he did, who would find him? The thoughts whirred round and round in his brain till his head also began to ache.

Andre took one last look at the ground, sat back against the trunk and decided to wait. He knew his father would come for him if he was absent another half hour, he told himself. Yes! His father would definitely come. He had to believe. Didn't Daddy always say he would look out for him?

Though the tears began to trickle out of his eyes, he stayed put.
He hoped and tried to think positively.

After what seemed like hours of waiting since he had left home (though it couldn't have been hours as the sun had not set yet), he heard someone calling out to him. 'Annnnddreeeeeeeee!' It was Daddy!

Andre hollered as loud as he could: 'I'm here Daddy, right here. Come soon! I'm waiting.'

He knew he was safe now.